The Haiku Bible

The Haiku Bible

Chris Suehr

RESOURCE *Publications* • Eugene, Oregon

THE HAIKU BIBLE

Copyright © 2012 Chris Suehr. All rights reserved. Except for brief quotations in critical publications or reviews, no part of this book may be reproduced in any manner without prior written permission from the publisher. Write: Permissions, Wipf and Stock Publishers, 199 W. 8th Ave., Suite 3, Eugene, OR 97401.

Resource Publications
An Imprint of Wipf and Stock Publishers
199 W. 8th Ave., Suite 3
Eugene, OR 97401
www.wipfandstock.com

ISBN 13: 978-1-62032-476-9

Manufactured in the U.S.A.

All scripture quotations, unless otherwise indicated, are taken from the Holy Bible, New International Version®, NIV®. Copyright ©1973, 1978, 1984 by Biblica, Inc.™ Used by permission of Zondervan. All rights reserved worldwide.

Contents

Old Testament

Mosaic / 3
Histories / 9
Wisdom / 23
Prophecy / 29

New Testament

Good News / 49
Pauline Letters / 55
General Letters / 69
Apocalypse / 79

OLD TESTAMENT

Mosaic

Genesis

God makes life from void
Deals with chosen humankind
Good, yet not perfect

Exodus

Freedom from Pharaoh
In wilderness, God provides
The Ten Commandments

Leviticus

Rites and laws of priests
Safety for nomadic tribes
Health, sense, and order

Numbers

Counts of roaming tribes
Fear and rebellions silenced
Promised Land is near

Deuteronomy

Forty years roaming
Moses presents laws and codes
Hear O Israel!

Histories

Joshua

Word leads in battle
Thirty-one kingdoms conquered
Promised Land harvest

Judges

God appoints leaders
To deliver from evil
No king in those days

Ruth

Widows flee famine
Ruth faithful to Naomi
Boaz delivers

I Samuel

Last of the judges
The people demand a king
Haughty Saul falls short

II Samuel

David anointed king
Sinful man declares Lord's rule
Nation under God

I Kings

Solomon's Temple
Rebel kings split North and South
Elijah speaks truth

II Kings

Elisha steps up
Evil kings lead to conquest
Temple burned and stripped

I Chronicles

Thorough history
From Adam to David's reign
Retells ideal times

II Chronicles

Reforming the kings
Prophets counter the wicked
Land gets Sabbath rest

Ezra

Cyrus writes decree
Displaced remnant returns home
Second Temple built

Nehemiah

First person reforms
City gates and walls rebuilt
Moses' laws restored

Esther

Exiled in Persia
As Queen, saves Jews from gallows
Lots of God at work

Wisdom

Job

A heavenly test
Does Job fear God for nothing?
Faith among ashes

Psalms

Broken seek refuge
Sing God's praise from peaks and pits
Rock and perfect light

Proverbs

Wisdom is from God
Folly is a bitter path
Wise to fear the Lord

Ecclesiastes

All is meaningless
Nothing new under the sun
Life is chasing wind

Song of Songs

Deep adoration
Beloved loves even more
See beauty in love

Prophecy

Isaiah

God with us enthroned
Will judge and restore the world
Light to all nations

Jeremiah

A voice young and wise
Sees disaster from all ways
Suffers showing signs

Lamentations

Jerusalem falls!
Rejection makes silent groan
Are we left alone?

Ezekiel

Alas disaster!
God will transplant your stone heart
Holy with purpose

Daniel

Heroic faithful
Braving kings in Babylon
Seeing the End Times

Hosea

Like a faithless whore
Ripped open by wild beasts
The torn will be healed

Joel

Locust invasion
Mourn for demolished harvest
The Lord shows pity

Amos

Plain shepherd seeks good
Sees first signs of wrath and hope
The fruits of justice

Obadiah

Rival brother lands
Jacob will burn up Esau
Zion is the Lord's

Jonah

Reluctant Prophet
Sent to save great Nineveh
Consumed with concerns

Micah

Down from high places
Woe and disaster await
God's mountain will rise

Nahum

God rules all nature
Nineveh will suffer wrath
They live like locusts

Habakkuk

God answers complaints
With unexpected blessings
Sing a song of awe

Zephaniah

All things swept away
The day of the Lord is near
Gather and seek God

Haggai

Build God's house again
Now lay a clean foundation
God seals the chosen

Zechariah

Visions to restore
Scattered to four winds and back
A new king will reign

Malachi

God beyond borders
The priests withheld true charity
New day will soon dawn

NEW TESTAMENT

Good News

Matthew

Christ is promised king
Fulfills Moses and Prophets
Reveals coming age

Mark

Suffering servant
Reigns and ransoms on the cross
Truly Son of God

Luke

A thorough account
Savior heals and sends Spirit
Seeking sick and lost

John

Word of God is light
Divine shepherd lifted up
The way, truth, and life

Acts

Spirit sends power
Mysterious Good News spreads
Through the divided

Pauline Letters

Romans

Death in old Adam
Right with God through faith alone
A new life in Christ

I Corinthians

Love community
One body is many parts
Sharing in Christ's meal

II Corinthians

Hearts veiled by false laws
Earthen bodies seek new clothes
Christ's glory unveiled

Galatians

Sent by Jesus Christ
But false laws cut themselves off
Gospel not from men

Ephesians

Christ marks by rich grace
Love in unified body
Love passes knowledge

Philippians

Bearing fruit in chains
Profit in Christ; Loss in laws
Endure and rejoice

Colossians

Christ holds cosmic rule
Set your hearts and minds above
Pray on and keep watch

I Thessalonians

Stand firm in trials
Lord, return with loud command
Night and day we pray

II Thessalonians

God brings full justice
The lawless will show false signs
One word will destroy

I Timothy

Expose false doctrines
Myths and fights leave shipwrecked faith
Leaders, be on guard

II Timothy

Rekindle your faith
Some oppose God's purposes
Preach in all seasons

Titus

Refute deceivers
Teach respect and self-control
Be washed in mercy

Philemon

Prisoners of Christ
The useless become useful
Slaves become partners

General Letters

Hebrews

Son shines God's brightness
Christ is priest and sacrifice
Pioneer of faith

James

Good deeds show your faith
Love your neighbors as yourself
Give yourself to God

I Peter

Hope will not spoil
Living stone builds a new house
Stand fast through ordeals

II Peter

Power of promise
Remember cleansing from sins
False prophets are blots

I John

Walk in word of life
Dark passes but light shines on
Love one another

II John

Walking in the truth
Loving others is not new
Christ lived in true flesh

III John

Be faithful children
Strangers become family
Goodness in the truth

Jude

Worms of corruption
Grace does not license to sin
Build on holy faith

Apocalypse

Revelation

Heed if you have sense
Behold cosmic majesty
First and last is God.